MW00901679

IDENTIFY   ACKNOWLEDGE   UNDERSTAND

Your
*Ø*ain Has
A Past

A GUIDE TO HELP YOU DETECT AND LOCATE
HOW YOUR PAST, PAIN IS HINDERING YOU FROM
LIVING YOUR BEST LIFE, TODAY

BELINDA S. ALLEN

Table of Contents

This Book is

---Dedicated to My Love, Emmanuel, my family, friends, and everyone that encouraged me to write. To every word spoken, of comfort, exhortation, edification and rebuke, Thank You.

The Journey began, remains and continues...

INTRODUCTION

Its safe to say that there are common denominators shared between humans, in the same way there are common qualities shared among all women or men. There are also similar experiences shared among generations like events, music, etc. We could also broaden our view and explore similarities of people within the same culture. However, the way in which a person process the moment could be very different.

You can take two people that were raised in the same home whose view of life were very different, both experience's were legitimate, but the affects, opposing opposites. We become a product of our processing based on how we perceived our life determines how we live our life. We make the mistake of believing that because two people shared the same experience their perception of the experience was the same. Similarities do not equate to equivalence, only the individual can elaborate on there mental process of that experience. The factors of why this happen can be based on age, race, sex, past experience, and the list goes on.

The emotional patterns that create our chaos and the pain that keep us stuck sometimes get buried under shame and embarrassment, this prevent us from acknowledging the severity of our issues. Most people would never admit or identify how their past has affected them, not because they don't want to acknowledge it, but because they can't see it. Many people know that there may be something unseen that is stagnating progress however, linking the cause is often the challenge. We tend to look at surface issues connected to what we feel we are lacking, lack of money, lack of opportunity, lack of support, lack of companionship, we fail to see our past pain as a culprit of sabotage. We tend to believe that if we had more of what we lacked, things would be better, however the truth can identify, if we had more of what we lacked, it still wouldn't be enough. The reason can be found in our inability to process the root of why we are in lack or in our interpretation of what we identify as lack. When we haven't dealt with the hurt, disappointment, regret, and pain of our past we measure our lack based on what we didn't have that others did. This becomes the present omen that keep us from arriving at our fulfilled self, and confined within a box of our ability to understand. The truth is, your past is affecting you, not because you are perseverating over it, but because you refuse to face it. Our emotions and its connections to moments in time has to be processed so that we can eliminate the emotional instability of our perception.

Our emotions work together, creating our process of elimination or the revolving door of a past in repeat mode. We either grow from our past or we repeat it. Most people are unaware of the influence their past has had on them, it's past pain that cause hesitation, an inability to finish, anxiety, competitiveness, and other behaviors that prevent healthy growth. Its pains triggers that control your actions and send you into caves to be tormented with fear of the unknown, fear of failure, fear of success or pride, it causes detours to progression and could lead you into unethical situations due to intimidation. Know that your emotions are either working for you or against you.

Acknowledging your truth can only determine what is true to you. Where has your emotions taken you? Your emotions are like a web woven, that will entangle you if not processed properly. Many who consistently live in the pain of their past, never learned the art of expelling and never saw the beauty hidden in their scars therefore they either work to forget their past or live within the confines of their past. It's important that we are aware that all pain is triggered, and It has a pattern. If you are are working through the pain to forget or living within the limits of pain, when you are dealing with mental, emotional and spiritual pain, it is easy to allow yourself to become driven in hiding its effects because of the fear of looking unstable. When you fail to deal with the pain of your past, it becomes the wall in your present and the curse of your future. It will show up in your relationships, in your children, in your emotions, and it can become the curse carried throughout generations to follow.

Most pain start off intense and dulls with time, an individual may feel something that doesn't feel quite right in a moment, but that feeling goes away after a while. It may have a span of weeks to several months and is usually tied to a more current incident that disturbed you. When the normal process of pain is interrupted, it is an indication that there is a deeper issue. Many times, we ignore the patterns of our pain in hopes that it will go away on its own. We must become more in tuned with our body response and willing to confront abnormalities. Our body will reveal that there is a problem, through physical body aches, extreme sensitivity, allergies, and other physical conditions. Our responsibility is to detect it's roots.

Pain is an indication that there is a deeper issue.

Intermittent Pain, may go away for a season but it comes back. This type of pain will show up on anniversaries of an event to remind you that you were hurt, or when you need to complete a task, to prevent results. This pain remind you that it hurt too bad to finish.

Chronic Pain, never goes away, you are constantly reminded that you were hurt, this type of pain torments you daily with negative thoughts of defeat, physical pain to keep you stagnant and spiritual pain to keep you hopeless.

It's true that time can heal, but only after you've pursued it with the intent to be healed. Your pain has a past that desires to keep you bound in turmoil and defeat and living within the confines of your thoughts-- you are what you believe. However, your pain also has a future end that must be pursued intentionally. It is during this pursuit, that you identify the growth in feeling weak and the strength in knowing that pains future is sealed in your truths actions.

In this book I will reiterate the point of dealing with your past pain, and offer help on how to work through negativity. It is my hope to guide you towards wholeness and educate you towards healing so that you can live your best life.

Chapter 1

YOUR PAIN IS A PROBLEM

Ask a person how they've arrived at where they are today, most people

can recount one pivotal moment and many recurrences of the same type of moment, that shaped their life. Though the truth of the effect of those moments resonates within our mind, it's roots were developed over time, intertwining with other emotions causing a soul disturbance. A soul disturbance is when something happens that agitate you emotionally, it's when your peace is disrupted. The effect of time did not process the journey effectively, but preserved every moment, storing hurt and suppressing pain.

Hurt is the effect of trauma, it is emotional damage as a result of the impact of trauma, trauma is a mental injury, it's memory scarring. Trauma occur when you witness or experience a situation that you attempt to understand and make sense of, but you can't. An individual may become mentally stagnant and confused, which affect how you feel. With trauma an individual may know that they have been affected but can't grasp the how or the why, the mind continues to seek to understand why you feel a certain way, keeping you as a prisoner to time.

Although the scars of being hurt may not be a physical scar, it can be visible through behavior, showing up in an individual being cautious in certain areas or in a persons unwillingness to be cooperative. You shouldn't feel the pain of scarring. Doubt and hesitation can cost you emotionally, they should not show up on your scar, preventing you from enjoying and being productive in life. A scar is only meant as a reminder and shouldn't be a block in the way of joy. There shouldn't be a reaction to certain issues that make you feel vulnerable and like a victim.

People stuff their emotions not realizing that, this process of stuffing is being stored within their internal hard drive that consist of the physical self, emotional self, and spiritual self. Stuffing will allow you to remain intact until you are overloaded, its effects will hide until the whole of you need to show up within a situation. These situations that requires your whole self are times of crisis such as a death, a divorce, health issues and other trauma. It's important that we realize that our body in its totaling nature and divine engineering has a memory, and life in its constant evolution, keep our bodies needing a systems cleanse because of our daily exposures. We were designed to store information and function within our design, however these daily exposures, to people opinions, stereotypes, prejudice, expectations, make us vulnerable to system failures, viruses, and difficulties making, it impossible to perform as intended with all of the other stored disappointments, failures, and rejection.

Most people are not aware that they have stored their hurt and suppressed their pain, and that they are experiencing hurt and pain related problem. We can identify the storing and preservation of our hurt and pain by examining our response to the thought of situations, circumstances, and events. What do you feel when you think about certain moments? The feeling of anger, bitterness, disgust, rage, or hate are emotional pain indicators of *not processing* the effects of an incident(s).

To help you identify if there are areas in your life that you haven't properly processed, I am providing a few descriptions of some of the emotions connected to pain. These emotions will invade your life, showing up at inconvenient moments, and disrupting your "normal".

Anger is an emotion that has to be awakened, it's not a first responder emotion, its aroused. There has to be something within your mental confinement that triggers it, passion compels anger to react.

Bitterness is an emotion rooted in resentment and unforgiveness, it keeps the memory of an event, current. Bitterness links everything that has happened in a person's life to one incident, keeping the person feeling that their life is the way it is, as a result of an event or a person. Bitterness hold on to offense and refuses to forgive.

Disgust is an emotion that cause a sudden physical reaction of feeling appalled and sometimes nauseous. Disgust may trigger anxiety or aches within the body. It causes a draw back from anything that may remind you of a person, place, or thing.

Rage is an emotion of being out of control, unable to tame your reactions. Rage is a brewing of your emotions fueled by anger and acts out destructively. Rage has to be satiated with an outward violent response.

Hate is an inward fury of hostility. It causes a person to be fixated on the actions of another. Hate expresses a strong prejudice towards a person's existence.

Anger, bitterness, disgust, rage, and hate are *expressive* and want revenge. They keep the feeling of hurt and offense alive.

The feeling of hopelessness, sadness, sorrow, and defeatism are emotional pain indicators of not healing from the effects of an incident(s). To help you identify if there are areas in your life where you ***haven't healed***, I am including a description to help you identify the lack of healing and emotional hinduraces.

Hopelessness is an emotion that gives you the feeling of not being able to accomplish anything. It steals your desire to try and causes you to focus on your inability to comprehend and envision results.

Sadness is an emotion that prevent a person from feeling happiness. It refuses to allow a person to live in the moment and enjoy life. It's a deep feeling of discontentment and projects the feeling of heaviness in thought and emotion.

Sorrow is the feeling of regret and extreme disappointment, its agonizing torment. Sorrow is an emotion that cause a person to feel like their soul is crying and moaning with utter grief.

Defeatism is the feeling of expecting the worse to happen. Defeatism is an emotion that evoke a bad attitude. The person seem to always have a problem with trying things.

Stoicism the feeling of being numb, unable to feel or show emotions, its repressive. The individual will feel not bothered and not affected by situations, good or bad.

Hopelessness, sadness, sorrow, defeatism, and stoicism are *inwardly tormenting*. They desire consolation, but they cause the person to isolate and feel pitiful and inconsolable.
Most people exemplifying this behavior, learned to repress and escape their emotions.

Hopefully, you were able to answer the question of, What do you feel when you think about certain moments, answering this question will help you to identify if you've processed and healed.

THE WEB

Identifying and Acknowledging where we are in our emotions is crucial to experiencing wholeness. It is important that we attempt to understand this web that our emotional instability create for us. The starting point of the web can be traced back to the string that you've attached to everyone that didn't meet your expectations and to everything that didn't produce what you felt you needed.

Pain is what you feel as a result of the hurt, it's your response to the impact. Pain forfeits progress and keep you stuck in the moment the hurt occured, pain is the reminder that you were in a wreck. Pain prevent growth and won't allow you to move beyond your hurt. Pain will paralyze your progress. This disposition of being stuck becomes a mindless act of a continuum, spooning a web that hold you hostage to your past. The webs connectors are every memory recall of disappointment throughout your life. Initially, meant as protection, over time the web becomes the trap used to kill your hope and passions, while paralyzing your progress towards your purpose and destiny. It's the pressure of pains strength that is used to squeeze and drain the life out of you. The web serves as a barrier that prevent growth and vitality, it doesn't allow your seeds of potential to be nurtured. It won't allow you to fill fulfillment, but discontent, nothing satisfies. Soon, your life become a journey of survival where you are trying to keep your head above water, rather than a journey of life.

The web keep you busy assessing your life in an attempt to not look like your hurt and preoccupied with suppressing pain and numbing your emotions. The web is self sabotage, it keep you guarded and defensive. Self sabotage is when you interfere with your own progress. It's design is meant to keep the real you concealed and the victimized you, exposed. It doesn't allow healing, because it holds you in a cycle of making poor decisions in relationships, job choices, etc. you become attracted to the pain that's living in you and addicted to dysfunction and the webs process until it start to take its course, distorting your view with the feeling of jealousy, thoughts of prejudice and resentment towards a person(s) and coveting what they have--- this could be in their personal possessions or their influence. The web will also distort your view with envy, a strong dislike and longing towards a person(s) personal possessions or their influence leading one into an attempt to deliberately sabotage the person they envy. Jealousy and envy will begin a spiraling effect of negative mental interference leading to stages of breakdown.

STAGES OF BREAKDOWN

The Denial Stage

You become a master artist in disguise, working hard to paint a picture of one having it all together, and being envied by others. However, it leads you on a never ending attempt to perfect your life to gain the approval of others.

Denial will keep you feeling like you are in control, it tells you, you could stop everything if you wanted.

Denial will not acknowledge areas of weakness, it protects you from the truth, that you are dealing with a problem too great for you to process and change.

The denial stage may include the following

Confusion - Having an inability to understand and come to a clear point of view.

Frustration - Feeling like things are unsettled and are headed towards a chaotic end.

Isolation - The person desires to be alone therefore they separate themselves from everything and everyone.

Paranoia - Thoughts of people speaking negatively of them. The person become overwhelmed with feelings of being unloved and out of control.

Emotional Outburst - The person have emotional tantrums, Crying spells, and feelings of being slighted that cause visible behavioral instability.

Private fits of rage - The person have sudden violent outburst that may include throwing things, pushing, aggressive cursing and gesturing.

Depression - Troubled feelings of wanting to give up or feelings of deep sadness and hopelessness.

Self medicating - Using substance or things to numb feelings such as drugs, alcohol, food, medication, sex, cutting, or anything used or done in excess. The danger of self medication is that it can be hidden under the guise of self reward, and control. It validates an individual with making them feel that they deserve the reward, and convincing them that they are in control and that they can stop when they choose -- its a tool of deception.

These emotions are no longer occasional visitors, but they play out in everyday life, an individual may experience a sudden release of tears because of mental frustration and fatigue. There may be adult tantruming about how life is unfair, daily complaints about people and how they aren't doing things right. Irritability because things are not perfect, constant comparison, and secret competitiveness, wanting to be the best at everything, becomes their drive. These seemingly harmless behaviors become more aggressive over time resulting in depression, poor relationships, health issues, mental torment, and internal conflict.

An individual may become stuck within their own web, unable to escape the life they've created. Although you may have experienced great success, it's never good enough, this web never allow the individual to live within the moment, but they stay actively perfecting the web keeping everyone far enough away as a way of protecting yourself.

Staying within the web will result in entering into a stage of great loss. Although the loss look differently per individual the affect is the same. **The Loss Stage** is where the individual may experience the following.

Loss of drive - procrastination and constant reasoning becomes the hindrance towards changing.

Loss of relatability - the person is unable to see things outside of their hurt, feeling that no one understands them, making it difficult for them to understand others. It causes an individual not to have sympathy for others, having an inability to connect emotionally with others.

Loss of meaningful relationships - the person may become judgemental and non tolerant of others. Becoming hypersensitive to motives, questioning the motives of people, as well as feeling like others don't want them around so they withdraw.

Loss of desire to work - the person may become passive in there level of excellence, refusing to perform at their ability because of disappointment and rejection. An individual may become consumed with thoughts of conspiracy and overwhelmed with expectations resulting in an individual impulsively quitting, constant calling in, and other insubordinate behaviors ultimately leading to them quitting or being let go.

The Loss stage promote feelings of not being able to get ahead, due to constant setback. The outcome of loss begin to brew an inward bitterness resulting in either a greater need to become better or a loss of will to live. Other times the need to please is greater than the need to care about what really matter. The pain of the past is a personality of its own, burying the person beneath the debris of hurt. The reactive response to hurt will program the brain to respond mindlessly to emotional pain--- this is why, an individual may perpetually do what they later regret, becoming entangled within the walls of instability and constant setback. The mind isn't aware that it's responding to past memory, the wound of yesterday is constantly being reopened by the encounters of today. Not dealing with the past is the knife that keep the cut fresh.

You have to crack the code of your reactive transmitters in order to respond differently to the hurt. Identifying where you are within the stages of the web will help you to stop these impulsive behaviors. Cracking the code, however, involves becoming aware of your behavioral patterns and their triggers. Our emotions are like security systems, a door must be opened before the system responds with an alert to turn the system off. You must find the door that's triggering your mental system and then you must switch it off. The alarm system doesn't sound the alarm unless there is an incorrect code entered or ignorance that a code is needed to turn off the triggered system. Unfortunately, many of us notice that something is wrong but we haven't identified the open door that's allowing our mental system to trigger our emotions. The door can be a person--- identify the toxic people in your life, or a place, there are some places that are attached to negative memories, or a thing--- it could be a piece of jewelry or an artifact. There are other things that may act as triggers such as smells, or dreams.

The code is the strategy used to stop the trigger, it is closing the door to intruders looking to steal your time, kill your purpose, and destroy your destiny, you may need to end a toxic relationship, take a different route to work or move out of that city. It may also require you to throw away an object, or stay away from a particular place, choosing not to view a certain film or refusing to participate in certain encounters with persons, may also be necessary.

Avoiding change is not an option, but a sacrifice that must be made, you must make a mental decision, a physical decision, and a spiritual decision to change each area providing a balance for the healing of the whole person. Make a decision to commit to your journey towards total freedom, your soul needs to be reclaimed from your past, and there must be an intentional pursuit, making emotional stability, mental clarity and a life of wholeness a priority. You can't continue doing what you've always done, but you must confront the past to free yourself from the web, or you will become prey to every negative word and every bad experience.

Stop living your life within the confines of how you feel, you will stay stuck if you allow your emotions to rule you. Identify and acknowledge that you have a problem, it makes it easier to confront the problem when you expose it. Understand, to feel and have an emotional reaction is not weakness, failing to deal with a problem is, its equivalent to running, stop running, and deal with your fear of looking weak.

You can untangle yourself from the web, when you make a choice to walk through those fearful valleys, those places of hurt and pain to get to the other side to greatness.

Chapter 2

CULTURE SHOCK

W e didn't have a choice in our culture nor our environment. Our

conditions were uncontrolled and predefined upon our arrival. We weren't given a choice but an opportunity to become greater than the life we lived, but the effect of our environment sometimes, become a lingering scent. Unable to get the stench of yesterday out, we become preoccupied with hiding from its effects instead of changing how we allow it to affect us. Often we become a subculture of our environment unknowingly, where we look different enough to distinguish us from our past, but our past is still embedded deep enough in us where it shows through our emotional instability. We are processed within a moral principle, subconsciously becoming a disciple of its laws, but we assume the appearance of our environment in one of its forms. We may become preoccupied with hustling because that was our exposure, we keep the mentality of our lack unknowingly. Our interpretation of not looking like where we came from becomes the fuel that drives us into dysfunctional behaviors.

As life happens we may find ourselves looking like what we hated and being enslaved to it, not knowing how to escape. An individual may desire freedom, but it seem unattainable, because the soul is tied to their past, causing a person to become developmentally stagnant and a carrier of abnormal behavior where we began to breed our dysfunction.

Within this subculture, we may have made it out from amongst "them" but the time spent with "them" has imprinted our soul. The handling of our life with the culture of our upbringing leave its fingerprints. This is why you can have a person who accepts most people but carry stereotypes. There decision to not hate others may distinguish them from their family, but their inability to judge character fairly is flawed by a perspective.

Everyone's culture is normal at its onset, which forge prejudice, it's not until a person goes outside of their norm that they see that there is a world outside of their own. Many times we are so acclimated to our "normal" that we are unable to embrace a universal culture of acceptance of others "different". This make change difficult to obtain, because our eyes are not accustomed to looking within to measure where we are. We fail to realize that although it's our norm, it's not a normal behavior outside the culture of our individual pain. You must acknowledge that your vantage point is keeping you stuck and unstable. You are able to identify the defect within your world when you are able to measure your life to the life intended for you to have. This can only be identified by comparing your life with the life predestined by God, for you. This predestined life goes beyond the life you desire for yourself--- Your destiny has been predefined and designed, it's tailored made for you by your creator. An individual must be willing to explore a realm outside of their own understanding to discover their greater self that's not habitat or socially centered--- it's your whole being having the capacity to align to a God centered purpose, it's your unique design fitted within this puzzled world.

Aligning to your purpose is having an understanding of the need for humility. *Humility* is having the willpower to resign from and divorce your past, its being real with the truth of your own inability to fix you and understanding your need for outside help. Its *Commitment,* being liable to your change and willing to endure the discomforts of being taught new behavior patterns. Its *Submission,* being willing to totally surrender to the God of change, and get under His mission for your life. Its having an *understanding* that your posture of change has an affect on your will to change, and your will to change is the determining factor if you change, this is a culture of its own, where creation returns back to its creator to learn it's intended purpose.

Many times we associate our pain, to failure, instead of to footprints designed to lead us towards a greater purpose, you were created for more and designed to endure the mishandling of life. You are weatherproof and fashioned to become more beautiful in the hands of time.

SHOCK

When we are being introduced to a culture outside our norm, an individual may experience shock. The change may cause a feeling of severe injury to your mental stability. Shock has what I believe are three potential reactions.

Stall (steal) - An inability to move, slow to transition. The stall reaction is aware of the need to go forward, but fear of the unknown hinders them from moving. This reaction is a thief of time, the persons failure to move prolongs change.

The way to break the stall reaction is to fall out of agreement with procrastination, set clear goals. Access how long you think certain processes should take and then set out to accomplish them.

Flight (kill) - To run without thought, forgetting where you came from, ashamed of your family. The flight reaction runs without weighing outcomes. The individual does not stop to explain their plan, they have a one track mind, to get out. This approach can damage relationships and may cause the person major set back because failure to appropriately disconnect.

The way to break the flight reaction is to pause and reflect on your progress so far, you must ask yourself the right questions to determine where you are, where you're going and the most effective way to get to your change. The flighty person would benefit from researching realistic timelines to accomplish their goals.

Reverse (destroy) - It cause an individual to stay stuck for fear of losing who they are or disappointing others. The reverse reaction is motivated by an individual's fear of disappointing others. This reaction destroys passion and drive towards change.

The way to break the reverse reaction is to identify the truth of your situation, and the reason why change is necessary. The reverse reactor would also benefit from determining a plan to help their family after they have embrace their change. It is important that this individual acknowledge that they have to set realistic goals for helping others.

FATIGUE

Commiting to change and deviating from what you've always known may also cause an individual to become weary. It's important to understand that just because you are making a decision towards change, it won't be easy. It is normal to experience the following symptoms of fatigue.

Physical fatigue - You are tired and desire to sleep, you have aches and pains without a diagnosable problem.

Overcoming physical fatigue will require you to push beyond your feelings and develop healthy habits. Schedule your day and commit to them, set small meaningful goals that you can accomplish. Change your eating habits, put more natural energy foods in your diet, eliminate mood induced foods such as sweets. The reason for the change is to invoke and reset your bodies natural body clock.

Mental fatigue - An individual may have brain fog, forgetfulness, and frustration.

Overcoming mental fatigue will require you to find time to relax. When we are going through processes of change, we tend to overthink what it should look like, we are wired with a desire to control and fix ourselves. Taking an approach of going on a journey rather then taking a runners sprint towards our change will help to settle our thoughts. Know that there are no unrealistic expectations in your process, one step at a time is all that's required.

Spiritual fatigue - An individual start to question what they've believed, and begin searching for something to validate their feelings. They will start entertaining compromising behaviors. An individual may also start to consider other spiritual avenues.

Overcoming spiritual fatigue requires you to return to basic principle. Settle in on the foundation of your faith and plant yourself in that, don't seek new revelation. When in a process, you become vulnerable and tend to look for the hole in your previous truth. Often times an individual may become confrontational towards that belief because of hurt. Therefore it's wise to find an "island" of truth and plant yourself there until you are rejuvenated in hope.

Fatigue can overwhelm you to the point of wanting to quit, you must keep going. Remember, if you have a willingness to change, you have the ability to change. What may seem to be your breaking point is really a ***deprograming*** of your culturally induced behavior. Your previous way of doing things is being forged out with the learning of a new behavior. It's also a ***rewiring*** of your perception, you are being stripped of tattered thinking and being replaced with new concepts and ideas.

Your change will have an influence on your culture. As you locate the roots of your dysfunction and model a new way, you will gain predecessor's that will desire to know how you overcame, they will help you to redefine your culture and stay committed to continued change. We oftentimes want to make excuses for our lack, but truth will define your starting point and maintain you to your finishing point. It's important to stay consistent, the more you practice a new way, the more you will merge to that new way.

COMMITTED TO CHANGE

Changing a culture, however, involves making sure that you understand how the culture began and the factors that resulted in the way things are, now. You must dig up the dirt covering the roots of your family's tree, to expose the foundation of pains past. This process is difficult because it will identify the seeds that were the culprit in aiding in your pain. We tend to think that our pain started with us, but you will be surprised to know that the result of your fate is buried within the lives of those before you. This may not be the case with everyone, however for most, if you examine the roots of your wounds in correlation to perversion, molestation, addictions, death, health issues within your family, you may discover a family history of these issues buried beneath pride and lies. The exposure of these truths are very fragile and delicate making it difficult to maneuver through without being forced to "shut up" from family that is too ashamed to admit the truth of their roots. It may involve the exposure of family secrets, or retracing family history and traditions that could have affected generations, this may also involve the revealing of curses placed on the family because of their involvement in cults, certain religious practices, group initiations, murder, exploitation, seance or mantras designed to alter the will. Understanding these roots will reveal the depths of what you're dealing with, which will uncover your, why, and provide you with the need to proceed. The significance in its exposure will bring clarity to a culture wounded and devoid of purpose, it will reveal the pain and the frustration that steered the actions.

People are programed and influenced into their way of life, your predator was once a victim of their environment. The environment is any place used to shape a morale, such as home, school, church. An individual is often held a prisoner in their thoughts and emotions that were shaped by what they saw, heard, felt, or interpreted through media, friends, family, associates or enemies. This is what germinated the seeds planted, which mean, anyone is a potential target and a victim of the conspiracies of life. There is no need to feel ashamed that you were a victim of a plot of fate, your past is proof of the existence of evil and the plan to forfeit your destiny, but your existence in today, is proof that their is a presence of good with a plan to defend you in evils plot of death and utilize your pain to perfect you towards efficiency to help others.

There is no optional plan to prevent confrontation nor is there room for excuse to remain confined to hopes convenience, you have to face the fears of your life's truths. You must break the cycle of rationalizing and protesting wrong through your silence. The reason is not to invoke messiness, but to implore truth. Through your process, wisdom must be applied, the objective is not to destroy the life of those living with the guilt of their actions or to deepen the shame within those who has kept silent, but its for understanding, to free yourself from the grip of the web.

Chapter 3

IT'S GOING TO HURT

Trying to understand the process of our pain is difficult. The complexity

of a conscience scarred is like attempting to retrace the steps of a web spun

by a spider who is deceased. The intricate detail of the web was spun in

time, following an innate process and creating a unique pattern that's hard

to retrace. The moments that caused our pain and spun our chaos are also,

too intricate to recall. It's not until we realize that the effects of time has

assassinated our purpose and marked us, damaged, no good and not fitting

for use. It strips away your worth and ties you to the lies of rejection,

rebellion, fear and stubbornness. Change, hurt, because its within the

process of change that we see how broken we are. The normal response to hurt is to set up protective barriers to prevent, feeling. These emotions that we use to protect, becomes the blockage that prevents progress. It is important that we are aware of the impairment that these emotions cause.

Rejection is your soul bleeding, leaving a stain on every area of your life. It deepens every wound and keeps it open and exposed. It won't allow you to heal, subconsciously causing you to lament as a victim to pain and a slave to your past. This gives birth to resentment and authorize discontentment to drive you into rebellion.

Rebellion is pay back, it's pain's way of regaining control while reconditioning your mind to believe the lie, that you're in control. Rebellion feeds on rejection and deceives you into thinking that you are choosing it, sending you on a self sabotage path of destruction, soon, pain marries with fear.

Fear builds a wall as a means to cope. It creates a unified system within your thought, emotions, and your body, in hope of protecting you from hurt. Fear will create an internal feud ultimately causing you to defend yourself, or mentally check out. Your worst enemy become yourself, because pain creates the delusion that everyone's out to inflict more pain. However, the real enemy is your perception, most people succumb to the ideal of being broken, incapable and too "messed up" to be effective in anything. The paralyzing of fear erects stubbornness.

Stubbornness is a forcefield, it is designed to protect the emotions from hurts possibility, it will not bargain, unlike the others, but is fixated on remaining in control. It refuses to be managed but is resolute in its protection, it disables all potential for growth. Stubbornness is passive in action, permitting things of importance to lapse, and having no motivation to follow through, but its aggressive in its unwillingness to change, in an attempt to appear in control of their life.

We create our mental world and paint it with our perception of our flawed self. An individual may unconsciously become obsessed with giving their pain a heartbeat by constantly feeding it with misconceptions and false truths of who they are. This mindset can only be broken when an individual detach themselves from their passion to keep the pain alive of constantly viewing themselves as small and insignificant. We must get clarity of our past and who we really are as defined by God, and take back the mental authority to think more of ourselves. Authority has to be taken back from the people that you gave up your power to. It will require resisting the desire to numb the pain--- you must process it appropriately. There must be an elimination of a need to feed rejection and rebellion and disconnect from a victim mindset, breaking the victim mindset is an intentional pursuit towards healthy thinking. The need to feed the victim in you will break when you choose to do the opposite of what your rejected self want to do in the moment. The victim mindset must be broken, the behavior has to be disciplined into change, intercepting negative thinking and behaviors at its onset.

The ways of a victim is a two sided coin, meaning, a person may fall under one who has truly been mistreated or one who use the victim behavior as a way to manipulate others and stay a victim. An individual must identify which truth is there's. Below I am providing a list of some of the behaviors of a victim.

Blaming Others,

Coin 1: This person refuse to take responsibility for their actions, They may have a mindset of "They made me do it" or they may look for the fault in others to prove that they are being victimized.

Solution: Identify the problem within situations and come up with three to four ways to handle the situation, weigh the pros and the cons of each, choose one. Seek out **wise counsel** for your decision--- someone who has a track record of making good decisions.

Coin 2: This person live with resentment towards their abuser to the point that everyone become their abuser. They associate their failure and their lack of progression to their offender(s).

Solution: Forgive the initial abuser, view people as individuals, take responsibility for your future. You may be a victim to your past but you are the steward of your today and the hope of your future.

Blaming yourself

Coin 1: This person lives in regret and believes that they are being punished for their past.

Solution: Acknowledge the consequences for your past and except that things may be more difficult for you but know that you have the strength to endure and you can break through all obstacles.

Coin 2: This person attribute their issues to something that they didn't do right. This person is a compulsive confessor that believe they are the problem in every situation.

Solution: Put the truth on your abilities and inabilities. You are not God nor do people expect you to be.

Comparison

Coin 1: This person is insecure and feel they are being treated unfairly. This individual look at other people lives and think, everyone has it better than them. They don't think anyone understand what they are going through.

Solution: Your life is what you make it, turn off the T.V. unplug your devices and get to know you. Guard what you hear and what you read, don't allow others to define the standard you are to live by.

Coin 2: This person feels entitled and that they are more deserving than others of success.

Solution: Focus on and appreciate what you already have and enjoy it, know that things don't make the person, the person make, the things. Work on becoming more humble, find a reason to be thankful everyday. Make a conscious decision not to compare yourself to others

Sabotage

Coin 1: This individual act helpless and is unable to progress because they refuse to do anything. This is the person that will not show up for an interview but complain of not having a job.

Solution: Do Something, don't call out, show up, do the opposite of what you want to do.

Coin 2: This person allow their rebellion to drive them, they are aware that they are rebelling and they want too. This person will purposely isolate themselves from help to prove that they do whatever they want.

Solution: Stop. You are aware of your actions because they are done on purpose. Fall out of agreement with the rebellious behavior.

Conspiracy Probing,

Coin 1: This person look for ill treatment, they always think that they are being overlooked and treated unfairly.

Solution: Stop looking for fault, anything and everything has the potential to look a certain way based on a person's perception. You must choose to look for the positive in every situation.

Coin 2: This person is very sensitive and think that things are being directed towards them. This person often feel offended by what someone said, because they believe that people have underlying motives.

Solution: Get a grip. Literally bring your emotions under subjection to the truth that everything is not about you, and even if something was about you, choose your emotions, don't hand over your stability to an opinion.

Sympathy Seeking,

Coin 1: This individual want pity, they want people to feel sorry for them. They often talk about how difficult their life is.

Solution: This person need to find reasons to celebrate. Everyone loves a fun person, people don't like to be around people that complain. Look for the joy in life.

Coin 2: This person use there sickness or ailment to bring them attention. When they are not the center of attention they will talk about how ill they are.

Solution: Discover purpose. Find someone to help, get involved, volunteer---helping someone else will help you feel significant.

Fear Finagling,

Coin 1: Exaggerating a fear of an outcome for attention. This person will speak of a desired outcome and say how difficult the task is and how scared they are of the task although they know that they can do it. They ask for help when they don't need help.

Solution: Be okay that you think that you can accomplish whatever you desire, it is false humility to stage the appearance of fear.

Coin 2: This person pretend to need the help of others although they know they can do themself. They display weakness for acceptance. This person doesn't want people to treat them different because they are good at many things.

Solution: *Be yourself, use your knowledge and ability to help others.*

Help Rejecting

Coin 1: This person talk about how helpless they are but refuse help because they don't want to "burden anyone". This person will allude to needing assistance but won't ask but will complain when no one offers to help.

Solution: *Ask for help if you need it. Don't hint, just ask if they say no, ask someone else.*

Coin 2: This person's pride keep them from receiving and asking for help when necessary.

Solution: *Know that people were designed to help when someone is in need. People want to help you, so let them.*

Victims are immobilized by their perception when they live within the lie of their battle. Being wounded in battle present the illusion of loss and affects our ability to see beyond where we are. The victim behavior is an attempt to gain control over weaknesses so the victim either succumb to there wounds by becoming passive, accepting things the way they are without making efforts to change or they seek to hide their wounds by becoming aggressive, provoking offense and refusing to change. Staying as a victim keep you as a powerless prisoner, stuck in the pages of a storyline of defeat. You must see the planning strategy of God in it all. You were created as a character in a heroic storyline who had to fight a villain but your end is victory.

Choosing to discipline behaviors that you have used to protect you will hurt the you that you've created but will help the you, you're becoming. Your life is destined to become a true life tale of triumph over trials. You may have been damaged, but you're not destroyed. Coming into the truth of who you are will present some challenges, you will have to fight and discipline yourself mentally, emotionally, and spiritually.

PAINS PRIDE

The major challenge that I have witnessed are those who started seeing a light at the end of the tunnel of their hurt, and therefore became prideful in their pain. This pride developed as a way to escape the appearance of scarring and as a result of seeing small victories. Pride can appear as confidence and motivation, however, the root of the confidence and motivation is connected to the advantage that the individual feel they have gained over their pain and their peers. The pride is fueled by delusion & deception, its a pipe dream from the effects of being down for too long. It is common for a person to shift from student to being completely unreasonable and unteachable. The person start to feel that they no longer need help from people who has helped them get to where they are. They find what they consider a more elite group to be around, forsaking friendships and community. The delusion blinds the individual from identifying with their real self as they pursue a life driven by their ideal self. This is a very dangerous position for an individual because they think they are doing the right thing based on how they feel, but they don't recognize this stage as part of their process of elimination, that's design to help them get rid of a false personality. This time is also dangerous because a person will roam around in this delusion for a period of a year before they realize that they are worse than when they began.

The stages of their delusion after they've seen the glimmer of hope generally start with the individual becoming discontent, they start talking to others about their discontentment who validate how they feel. The individual becomes deceived by a self induced revelation that they are great and others can't see them for who they are, the individual start to feel that the process has been taking too long and they could heal faster without the help of others. The person becomes fueled by there false confidence and become motivated by self sabotage, the person disconnects from there help and enters into, what I call, an Altered Reality.

This Altered state causes the individual to make drastic decisions, the deception keep them motivated to stay disconnected and the delusion keeps them focused on self.

Three to five months into this Altered reality, the individual slowly start coming down from their high, and start to question their decisions, within the **fifth month** they begin to recognize the seriousness of their decision,

month six they start to feel stuck, **month seven** they are too embarrassed to admit that they made poor decisions, and seek to hide it. **Month eight** the individual makes an attempt to start over, they may try to get back into counseling and reach out to others. **Month nine** they feel like they are making progress again, **month ten** they are really trying to adapt to their new environment, **month eleven** they are feeling like everything is chaotic and start to notice that things are not the way it seemed. They start to recognize the presence of deception. **Month twelve** the individual goes back to living there life the way they want, attempting to forget the progress they had made prior to their deception and delusion, adopting the belief that nothing and no one was able nor capable of helping them effectively. The person then seeks to protect their decisions by building a stronger wall of pride although they are in pain, replacing their pain with privilege instead of with purpose. Their priorities become self centered, self rewarding and self gratifying inducing a heart inflamed with prides behaviors. A person exemplifying characteristics of pride may operate in the following behaviors.

Judgmental - forms an opinion based on a person's circumstance.
Fault finding - look for areas of weakness in others and highlights them.
Entitlement - feel that others owe them honor.
People Pleasing - does things for the approval of others.
Confrontational feel that it's their responsibility to correct others or put others in place.
Attention Seeking - does things to be noticed.

Unteachable incapable of receiving from others. This person feel like they are the expert and refuse to hear other ideas or opinions. They believe that they are always right.

Self Serving - only concerned about their own interest and what is important to them.

Materialistic/Superficial - give much attention to how people see them on the outside

Self Righteous - feel like they don't have to answer to anyone. This person refuse to show honor and believe that they are the superior.

Humility, choosing to think of yourself less and consider others more is the only way to combat pride. The desire for power over our pain and control over hurt is the bait that draws pride. Pride shows up to deceive an individual into believing that they are getting better, it is confidence evil twin. An individual must identify the presence of deception lurking within the time between hope and healing, camouflaging as knowledge.

There is a predestined plan, written by our creator, God, that we can submit to or forfeit with our own plan. Our plan place us in the hands of fate. Fate is the result of life happening to us because of our failure to submit to God's plan that work all things out for us. There reside only two laws of life, you can live with purpose or die with destiny still locked up on the inside of you, you choose, through your commitment towards change.

The damage from past pain is propositional, a change of perspective can help you see it's worth. The value of anything is within the eyes of the beholder, our scars add value, when we change our view, and when we

47

identify pain's purpose. Our process should help us to see the beauty in our scars, and not the damage of our pain. Change hurt, but setback and hindrances hurt you more. Don't allow your mistaken identity keep you from pursuing the greater you, seek to find the error within your inflated mental system. Our emotions are constantly sending signals for us to deal with our errors, that we tend to override, choose to remedy them. Reroute yourself, you must decide to start the process, again, you're worth the inconvenience. Remember you are investing in your wholeness, allow the work that you started to continue until your change is complete.

Chapter 4

LEVEL UP

W e are creatures of habit and adapters to environments, it's how we

sustain and cope. The continuity of our life in motion program our
cognitive development, compiling a database of responses. The more we
practice behaviors, we start to perform those behaviors in our everyday,
they become habits locked into our memory, happening without intention.
Processing is a method of intention, it requires identification,
acknowledgement, understanding, confronting, filtering and letting go.
This assures that you effectively break down how your mind stored the
event(s) in your memory. Processing allow you to breakdown the hard
facts of any given situation and convert it into purposeful information that
can be used to make you better.

It is important that we understand pain in its context, pain is purposed to alert that something is wrong, its trigger is a tool of detection. It's designed to compel an urgent response to locate and fix the problem, however, pain's significance goes beyond a physical sensation, it can also be mental pain, from grief and torment. As with physical pain, mental and emotional pain detects a problem then alerts you with feelings of being vexed, and overwhelmed by feelings of hopelessness, regret, sorrow, remorse, heartbreak, and misery. All have felt pain but we expect to grow beyond our pain, having the ability to distance ourselves from the thoughts of the past, but there has to be an intent to process it.

The aspects of pain are designed to invade, disrupt and alert you, processing pain properly will help to prevent pain from perpetuating. Processing is *identifying* when something has hurt you, and *acknowledging* its effects in your life so that you can expose it and prevent the hurt from lingering. It is *understanding* that you have within you, the ability to overcome. know that you already survived the worse, you lived through your experiences therefore you can progress beyond where you are.

Processing will open up locked doors of opportunity that fear has kept you from possessing and will free you to be your authentic self, giving you permission to become who you were meant to be. It is important that you give yourself permission to feel raw emotions and *confront* them through self examination. Be honest about how you felt at the moment that the offense occurred and *filter* through the truth of your emotions, separating the truth from the lie you believed, and removing all of the negativity that invaded your thoughts and kept you feeling hurt and in pain. There are specific thoughts that invade our emotions and keep us bound. These negative thoughts tend to fall under, assumption, which creates a false truth, that exist without validity. It's often tied to a perception based on our ability to understand the why of a situation. What we believe shape our world, we manifest what we presume as truth, and react in defense of our belief. An individual's actions are a reaction of their processing. An emotion such as bitterness is fostered out of presumption and is rooted in an inability to understand the purpose, it is unrelenting hostility.

EMOTIONAL PROCESSING

An individual must learn to to see life from different points of view, seeking understanding to assist in breaking down the wall of false truth to see accurately.

It's important that you understand the stages of your emotions so that you are aware of the emotions that you need to **let go** of. Note: Anger is a partnering emotion, meaning, you feel an emotion prior to anger. However, most people try to deal with the most insistent emotion, because it's the most expressive, but the root is the emotion that is most docile, anger is custodial. Its protective nature seem to be the dominant emotion because of the visible behavior that may come with anger. The thought is to seek anger management when that's not the root problem. I will give you an example...

Example 1: The situation: When you were five your dad said that he was going to pick you up and never did, your mom started to notice that you went from being a really sweet kid to an angry kid.

If we were to process this scenario appropriately, we would first identify the problem, then the emotions connected to the problem, and attempt to understand the details of why you felt the way you felt.

The problem: dad did not pick you up

The emotions:

1st **sadness** because dad didn't come.

2nd **disappointed** that he didn't call to let you know that he wasn't coming

3rd **frustration** because you couldn't do anything about it, and mom couldn't understand

4th **anger** because you were tired of crying and feeling at a lost, and you wanted to protect your feelings.

It's crucial to *Acknowledge* how you really felt in the moment. The challenge in acknowledgment is that it forces you to feel, again, what the anger prevented you from feeling. To ease the pain of the truth of your emotions, allow yourself to say what you wanted to say in that moment of the offense, out loud. The power in doing this saturates your world as you knew it, with the truth of how you were affected by your dad's absence and failure to follow through. Ask yourself the hard questions like, why didn't he show up, and seek to understand the why? The answer may come from asking him directly, why he didn't show--- be willing to accept whatever

52

answer he gives without wonder, he is responsible for his own truth. We may also need to assess the truth of his life at that time. Was he a user of alcohol or drugs, did he have another family, was he mentally unstable or irresponsible, did he have a relationship with his father? After assessing, and seeking understanding, you will need to process the details. If he was a user of alcohol or drugs, he was unable to make informed decisions because of the effects of the drug or alcohol use. Research the behaviors of a person under the influence of drugs to get a better understanding. Maybe he was just ignorant or selfish, the truth should free up your emotions to know that his issues had nothing to do with you, but it was his own sickness or his ignorance, not knowing how to properly problem solve that robbed him of time with you.

You must know that your worth is not tied to someone else behavior. Next, you want to *forgive* him, forgiveness is you choosing to *remove* the chains from your emotions and the mental torment in your thoughts of not being good enough or worth his respect. *Confront,* within yourself, how their actions affect you, and let go of the right to be angry.

Example 2: The situation: You have been feeling down lately, unmotivated and tired. You seem to have everything that you need and what others want, but you feel like life is happening without you. You are noticeably depressed, but don't know why.

The problem: you are not happy with your life
The emotions:

1st **discontentment** you may have saw something that you wanted, and you coveted it and compared your life and felt that your life didn't measure up
2nd **disappointed** your life doesn't look or feel like you imagined it would.
3rd **sad** because you feel unfulfilled and unhappy
4th **lonely** you feel like no one understand what you are going through, and you miss the fun you use to have
5th **frustrated** because you feel helpless and overwhelmed with responsibility
6th **depressed** because you feel stuck without a way out.

Acknowledge that you are not happy with your life and that you are disappointed at how your life has turned out. Acknowledge how you expected for your life to be and confess the choices that you may have made that were poor, that could have contributed to your pain. Remind yourself of the reason that you made your decisions. Remember what was going on in your life during that time and how it made you feel. Ask yourself why you regret it, now. Discover what you are measuring your life too, ask yourself are they needs or wants, and why. Know that the secret to satisfaction is in understanding whats sufficient, and live within the means of enough. It takes repurposing your life within the limits of what you already obtain, knowing how to live substantially within your resources. Fantasy may be driving the disappointment, adjust your interest, think within your reality and get around others whose reality match yours and are content. Spend time growing those healthy relationships, share ideas with people who value your now, and who share common interest in organic growth. Life is a journey, enjoy it, shift your view of you, live in your now, and set realistic goals with steps to follow through.

The truth in these moments are the past that will free you and alleviate the pain. Your past pains truth is stuck in the real emotions of a moment that you didn't want to feel. The truth will free the caged bird within yourself, giving you permission to move on from yester-years distorted truth and soar into today's possibility. Your destiny, is greater than a momentary disappointment. Truth will always free you and help you to quickly let go of the opinions of others and the need for approval and validation. It will release you from the torment of rejection and the sabotage of rebellion. Process every moment that you have attempted to bury and start to identify your pain patterns--- the stages that your emotions go through that lands you into your emotional prison. Pain's patterns exposes the severity of a traumatic experience. Be willing to be transparent, and ask yourself the right questions to determine pains onset. Many times we are just trying to go through but God want us to grow through it.

GROW THROUGH IT

Growing through our pain is learning the lesson. The lesson is not taking on a defensive protective role that you can't trust anyone, but its allowing yourself to develop a greater compassion for others. The truth that we often miss is that most people suffer from trauma, and are trapped at the scene of an experience. Growing through involves character building, its when the core of who you are mature in the area that you were hurt. It's a process of refocusing, you no longer see yourself as a victim, but an overcomer. Develop your processing system, refusing to allow pain to keep you hidden within the pages of time.

The development of this new system of processing will take some getting use to. All organic and healthy growth occur with compliance, patience, discipline, consistency and commitment.

Compliance, having a willingness and a desire to follow through with the demands of a process.

Patience, having the right attitude to remain stable and the endurance to wait and be tolerant of the problem

Discipline, being determined to finished, restrained in your desires and integral in your obligations.

Consistency, faithfully practicing healthy processing, without deviating from or compromising

Commitment, being dedicated and loyal, its making a promise to finish

Change demands your attention, it's being willing to put in the work to reap the results you need . There are no off days to this process, it must become a lifestyle or you will fall back into your old patterned behaviors.

This process requires your active participation, stay alert, don't check out. Avoid the desire to escape, beware of compromise, procrastination, fantasy and endless planning.

Compromising thoughts entice you to adjust your regimen and tell you that it doesn't take all that.

Procrastination will tell you that you can start another day

Fantasy is lazy behavior that keep you wishing but doing nothing

Endless planning keep you occupied with an idea, you stay in a cycle of "trying to figure it out". You may have blueprints, vision boards, books etc., however you are stuck. The key to ending, endless planning is to, just do it, if you don't have the tools you need by now, you're not going to find it, starting is your only option.

Change doesn't come without strategic intent, it must to be pursued and nurtured. Your roots have to grow deep enough within a renewed mindset to stabilize you for every season of your life. Refuse to hand your authority over to your emotions, don't elect & release power to negativity, but guard your sanity with truth. Know that you are either filtering or fueling your emotions and that truth must be the reminder that keep you persistent in your processing. You will have many days of readjusting, adapting to your changing environment, but remember, a temporary inconvenience is worth a life freed to live.

Chapter 5

GET OUT

I understand that your wounds have roots, and that there's no quick fix to

the mental torment that you've felt, the mask you've worn for years, the excuses that's become your escape, the denial that's kept you sane, or the avoidance that's made you feel protected. You may feel you've made attempts to change the effect that your past has had on your life, trying to search your soul, think more positive and do the right thing. As a result you may feel *physically exhausted,* having little to no energy to complete daily task, *mentally drained*, having no ability to reason or rationalize, *emotionally frustrated*, confused and tired of life as you know it, because of the lack of progress you've made. You may feel like nothing has worked and you are tired of pretending, you've been holding on to hope and believing that things are going to turn around, but it hasn't. You must change your method, your way of doing things, it's Insanity to continue to do the same thing repeatedly with no results. Find the doorway out of pains past, that's holding you hostage, get out of a mindset contaminated with wrong thinking and actions. You can't trust the victim in your mind, encouraging you to defend your pains behavior. Find your roots within the soil of chaos and acknowledge who you've become, embrace what's true about you.

PERSONALITY CONFLICTS

It takes time to uproot a tree and repair the damage of a compromised foundation, but it's not impossible, however, denial and avoidance prolongs the process. Pain has a way of tainting our view, misleading and blinding us with delusions, causing us to become fixated on a mirage, where your desert life start to look like a stream of life. An individual may start to believe that they are growing and getting better when they are dying and falling apart. Delusion may cause an individual to mistaken a web for a cocoon, trapping them in a season, and suffocating them with oppression, prolonged torment.

Getting out involves identifying the personality that dominates your life and keep you stuck, and applying a new approach out of your mental confinement. Often times it's not that an individual doesn't know what to do or is unwilling, but they are unaware of how to do it with the hindrances attached to their specific personality.

It is my hope to help you maneuver through the challenge of who you are by providing a description of a personality type, the hindrance attached to the type and a strategy to help you be effective.

Personality one: Those that want to change, but need some enforcement. This individual is unmotivated and don't like to be inconvenienced. You are unable to make the right mental choices, your appetite drives you, you are able to operate in restraint but your double mindedness keep you battling mental torment. You are the compulsive thinker, you think of an excuse to get out of doing what you know is right. Your primary issue, is your failure to get help because your pride won't allow you. You know that you are weak but refuse to acknowledge your weaknesses.

IMPLEMENT: Commitment *(see chapter 4)*

Personality two: Those that are motivated to change.

You are the person who is quick to make changes, but also quick to put someone else down. Complaining, fault finding, self awareness and intolerance are your enemies. They will keeps you occupied with others which prevent you from working on just self. You have the inner motivation to change but you are a manipulator of systems, you become too busy to change. You are also preoccupied perfecting outside changes and too critical to allow anyone else to help you. You will prefer to do it on your own.

IMPLEMENT: Patience *(see chapter 4)*

Personality three: Those who don't want to change but know they need to change

You live your life not wanting responsibility and blaming others for your life. Your life has been arrested by trauma, you refuse to move beyond your pain. You are constantly in search for someone else to assume the responsibility. In relationships you are selfish, neglectful, and ungrateful. You have the challenge of being too faithful to your pain, using your traumatic past to buy you more time to prevent from changing. Your pain is your friend.

IMPLEMENT: Discipline *(see chapter 4)*

Personality four : This person is stuck, clueless, indecisive, unable to see the truth of their situation and the effects it's having on them. Nothing applies to this person, they have managed to convince themselves of their own lie, that they are okay the way they are. This person is certain that people are the problem, they believe that others need to change to understand them.

You are the perpetual soul searcher. You have studied how to be you. You made yourself into who you are. You have developed an alter ego and found your own inner peace, but your enemy is regret. As life progress you regret certain life choices because of the trauma of your past, you choose your escape. This person thrives on success and becoming better, you are addicted to making up your own rules. You live outside the confines of what people think of you. You don't trust anyone, making it difficult to build new relationships.

IMPLEMENT: Compliance *(see chapter 4)*

Bonus fifth Personality : This individual have bouts with each of these personalities, making it impossible to finish anything. Your inability to stay consistent keeps your world in constant unproductive motion. Your constant instability keep you in a cycle of starting over.

The Bonus Fifth has no true identity. This person seeks out common ground with everyone deceiving themselves to thinking that they are just like another person.

IMPLEMENT: Consistency *(see chapter 4)*

Whatever life has groomed you to be, you are not your past. It may take some time to deprogram the mental barriers in your perception, but you can change. Your change start with a decision to overhaul your life, replacing your personal personality conflict with deliberate action. There may be drastic decisions that you may need to take to get rid of the peace disruptors, the people place or things that birth chaos in your life. It's impossible to live in a house full of trash and not smell like it. Refuse to be around people and their drama. You must take back your emotions and stop the storm, if it causes negative feelings to resurface, stay away.

PROPER CONNECTION

Its difficult for people to understand the extent of your pain and your need to disconnect as you heal. For instance, you may want to visit your mother, but if she lives in the house where you were sexual abused, it's okay to stay away for a season. You will need to let mom know how you feel, and own your feelings. Don't allow her perception to make you feel like you're overreacting. Take the power back over your life and explain to your mom that you're on a journey towards wholeness and that you are unable to visit her until you work through your emotions. Make arrangements to commit to calling her, or meet over coffee, breakfast etc. away from the home or have mom visit with you at your home. Discover ways to spend quality time, but in an environment that doesn't ignite mental instability. The same intentions must be pursued with other family and friends, know your mental limits and create safe boundaries until you heal wholly. The reason for creating these boundaries are solely because of how our lives are affected by memory, you are a body that's alive, full of electrical currents.

Some would define this phenomenon as "energies" or "vibes" however, my expression would be "spirit" we are tri part beings consisting of a spirit that naturally flow through the body that can be affected by negative and positive energy/ spirit producing elements, people, places, things and it naturally respond to the currents they release in atmospheres. This is why you can be in certain places or around certain people and not have a good feeling or why you can enter into a home and are triggered. You can even drive in a neighborhood and feel uncomfortable because your surroundings frequency has been manipulated by the dominating spirit of a place. The presence of these spirits within our environments have the ability to breed life or retrieve life, you must make sure that you are guarding the life in you and setting up hedges to contain your world for considerable results. The energies/spirit in places are the life of a place, a dominating personality alerting you of what has taken place within that environment that can influence or trigger a behavior or a feeling. We are spiritual beings with an ability to connect with a spirit world that enables us, giving us authority and permission or disables us, limiting and immobilizing our ability to function within reason. Your power to think, understand and react are powered by a God source, and empowered, given a greater capacity to thrive and overcome through our connection within that greater source. You must make sure you are connected to the right God source, because the wrong god source will multiply chaos in your life causing confusion and delusion. We must be aware of the potential for manic invasion that will strive to influence you into a demented hysteria and forced compromise.

The correct God connection is often interrupted by what's happening around us, these outside sources outage power out of our life, and contribute to our disconnect. You must identify where you are losing power and the source(s) that are draining you and cut ties. Your understanding of how environments contribute to dysfunction will allow you to see the unseen traps that are waiting to hinder your change, don't be ignorant to the presence of evil conspiracies and blackout, a failed surge that prevent motivation and movement. Be willing to disconnect from what's tripping your emotional power switch and restore a greater connection to the God source who will help you endure the process and change your life.

TRAUMA

In the case of a diagnosis of mental illness, I believe most mental illness is triggered by trauma resulting in an inability to cope with the process of life. I am not a professional therapist or psychologist of any sort, but I have had many encounters within my profession, working with the SMI (seriously mentally ill) community as a case manager, counseling and life coaching non professionally, and interacting with people as a whole. I have noticed the same patterns regardless of the individual being diagnosed professionally or personally, trauma is often the culprit, with drug abuse being the close second, which is linked to trauma as well.

I believe mental illness is due to a faulty mental composition of thoughts and behaviors. The mind goes into a mental block mode as a way of dealing with trauma resulting in an inability to process effectively, it's a false personality that a person adopts as a result of attempting to cope. I have noticed a pattern of illness/disorders that are commonly associated to the following traumas, other factors can apply, however I will provide a general perspective, again, please note, these are based on my personal observation and does not represent the views of a professional.

Depression specific disorders - perseverating on the results of an incident, a decision or a lack and feeling helpless in changing it.

Anxiety specific disorders - fear of the unknown, failure, success, people, places, etc. It's a triggered behavior normally in connection with a situation or an incident, an individual may have felt out of control. When an individual feel that they are in a situation that seem to be spinning out of control it produces a reaction of panic.

Post traumatic specific disorders - memory recall of an incident that your mind and your body remembers. It could also be connected to wanting to go back in time and change your response to an incident to prevent it or protect.

Obsessive compulsive specific disorders - the need for control, wanting to control your environment, how people feel about you etc. It's connected to perfection, feeling that perfection is more acceptable. It may also be linked to a past memory of not feeling good enough or at a disadvantage, therefore you seek to control your environment.

eating, drug, and sex abuse specific disorders - the need for pleasure, escape, satisfaction, and control, commonly connected with being abused, neglected, and abandoned. It's the way a person seek to control their feelings and need for love. It's mental aggression to dominate over the pain of mistreatment.

In the case of *eating* the person indulge until feeling full as an indication of satisfaction, an individual may have used food as comfort because they felt abandoned or they restrict as a form of control or punishment from self hate.

In the case of *drugs* the individual desires to gain control over their life and becomes passive in wanting to escape and aggressive in feeling like they are taking control, and doing what they want.

In the case of *sex* the individual desires pleasure as a way to escape or gaining control over their life to prevent from in feeling like they are a victim. They choose to satisfy their need for love by compromising their body. This individual may have been sexually violated so they become the

66

aggressor or they may have been abandoned and they use sex to compensate for a lack of love.

dissociative disorders - a way of disconnecting from reality and escaping. It's stress induced, and rooted in not wanting to deal with life. This is the individual that may not be able to stay awake, or who "check out", as a way of coping. This individual may create a fantasy world or use other things like games or shopping to avoid dealing with reality.

I believe that proper processing can eliminate the pains and disorders that are present as a result of attempting to cope. It's choosing to live, finding purpose and peace and not just existing and becoming a product of fate. I believe that the possibility of healing is greater when we understand the root of issues.

Chapter 6

PICK UP THE PIECES

Ｉt's one thing to be foolish, lacking caution, wisdom, and understanding

but another thing to be deceived, mislead and falsely persuaded and
misguided, in the case of our past pain the two *Foolishness,* the inability to
judge situations wisely and *Deception*, being mislead, seem to work
together. It's the pain of their existence in our past that keep us vulnerable
to pain. It's difficult to overcome a painful experience when you're unable
to assess and implement a solution and when you are unable to see the
truth. You must push the reset button on your life and get into a position to
attain healing, getting rid of the mental resistance and choosing life, your

pain has a purpose. Your pain got you here, robbing and emptying you of a fulfilled life, and you must force pain to compensate you. Your payout happens when you become desperate for change, utilizing principle to help you find your way out of a life of pain. The purpose in your pain is not a ploy of deception to keep you from acknowledging truth, but it's the acceptance of meaning and the understanding within reasonable thought. It's an art of intention, having the ability to change your resolve, it's concluding to learn the skill of prevailing over defeat and mastering finessing the pain out of your past.

The pain yields success when you fight to change, you must stop pain from happening to you and make it work for you. Make a conscientious choice to not give up. Interrogate the life out of instability and compromise. Question your thoughts, feelings and actions holding them up to the light of truth to reveal unhealthy processing. Pick up the pieces of your defeated seasons by revisiting the moments in your past where you left your mind, body, and soul and recover all. There must be a forbearance tenacity to see results and live a better life. You must discover your will to live. Hne a purpose driven indignation, ignite desperation for freedom from torment taking on the characteristic of one in panic mode. The principles within the panic mode will help you out of your "tight spot" moments, it's your exit strategy

PRINCIPLES OF PANIC

Principle one: Expose secrets
*Secrets are an action of fear

The bitterness of words unspoken help to keep the pain alive. You must come clean, and confess to someone who is a trusted source. There is healing in your confession.

Principle two: Renounce involvement
*Our involvement in continued cycles are indicators of evil invasion

Break the curse of being a victim, by realizing that you have allowed other people to control you. You must gain control over your own emotions and decide to choose your own feelings. Refuse to hand over your power to another to control how you feel. Take back your emotions, refuse to allow yourself to feed your past with regret, resentment, and bitterness, they keep pain alive, because they nourish your rejected feelings and your rebellious actions. You don't have to continue to relive your past, divorce it. Take back your right to choose what affects your tomorrow.

Principle three: Surrender Control.
*Feeling in control is our attempt to solve a problem

Rebellion seeks to gain control while spinning you out of control. Rebellion is a soul manipulator, it tricks you into believing that you are doing what you want by becoming more victimized through self harm. Rebellion is toxic to your life, it poisons the body while manipulating the

70

mind to think that it's punishing someone else. It's you drinking the poison of self destruction and expecting the other person to die.

Principle four : Face It
*Choosing to stay hurt is connected to Stubborness

Often times we feel like we have a right to be hurt, there is a sense of satisfaction that comes with feeling that you are punishing a person by not forgiving them.

The power in choice is the forced exhalation of breath being put back into your life. It's the will to live when it's too painful to live. It's the dispelling of your minds perception being trumped by what really matters. In the case of crisis, purpose and destiny must become the propellant. Everyone has a purpose that is meant to lead them to a destination. The extent of that purpose will only go as far as the persons revelation, having an understanding of that purpose. A person's willingness or capacity to understand that purpose will either lead them into a life lead by fate or destiny.

Fate is when life happen to you, life is taking its course as a result of decisions made, that are linked to decisions that someone else made that affected you, decisions that you made as an act of rebellion, or both. Most people decisions are fueled by there rejection, meaning unprocessed pain is driving their behaviors. It's important to acknowledge that Most, implies that it's possible that your life is a result of fate, which is inevitable when you don't know your purpose. The only way to pry yourself out of the hands of fate is to discover your purpose, know the path that you are to take to get there, and progress forward, refusing to look back.

Destiny is the destination which consist of directional elements before arrival. There are components that are hidden within the creator that can only be activated through proper connection, you must know the truth of your life and that truth will free you from the pit of life into the path of promised prosperity where you are liberated to live your best life as purposed by the creator. A creator always has a purpose for its creation, birthed out of a need for its existence. You are needed to show up in your destiny, your future is depending on you.

The joy of life is in knowing why you yet live, the significance of now, is that everything that you've experienced can be used as a piece within this puzzled life. Even if you hadn't thought about your reasons why until this point, and you feel like you are in a race between time, know that it's not too late, you can finish well, ending at your destined place. It's not a matter of loss but of gain, what have you gained from your life, what do you know now, that you didn't know then? Don't focus on your failures, think of the lessons you've learned and talk about it. "No Regrets" has to become the sum of your story, the lessons learned has to become the glue that mends you back together, and fulfilment has to be the hope that resets your life. You can't undo what has already been done but the significance of change is about changing your futures outcome. You can't die as a captive. There is greatness inside of you, a gift given to you by God, you can live a life of joy.

Chapter 7

INTENTIONAL BREAKTHROUGH

Y our pain was not meant to outlast your purpose, but should be the

vehicle to catapult you into your destiny, your season of pain has to pass. There is a season to everything, the key is learning to thrive in every season. We must become like trees that have learned the art of seasonal change and how to embrace seasonal purpose. This is a challenge for most because it require you to break the pattern stored in your memory. You must relearn how to live outside of what you've always known. This process, hurt, and becomes frustrating because it requires you to push past the pain of being in a place of unfamiliarity. It's beneficial to know pain, but not to live in it, embrace seasonal change and refuse to remain in seasons longer than intended. There is purpose in every season, learn to weather the seasons by being intentional in each season, it's important to recognize the seasons that you are in so that you know how to get the most out of them.

WEATHERING YOUR SEASON

Winter Season: a time of isolation and rest. In this season reevaluate your circle of friends and distinguish those that are an asset from those who are a liability.

Do: say goodbye to toxic relationships, prioritize your time, stay motivated

Beware: of people who would want to take up too much of your time, and picking up old habits. Don't give in to feelings of rejection

Spring Season: a time of growth and development. In this season meet new people who you can benefit from. Enroll in a course or attend a seminar

Do: welcome new ideas, be hopeful, intentionally mature, stay alert

Beware: of counterfeit relationships, gimmicks, and time wasting activities and or people. Verify your information to avoid being deceived.

Summer Season: a time of new experiences and testing. In this season enjoy life and try something new. Be willing to make necessary commitments to obtain consistent results.

Do: enlist help to keep you stable. Take healthy risk, stay focused and listen to wise counsel

Beware: of becoming irrational and rebellious. Remember you are still in a process towards wholeness.

Fall Season: a time of loss and being rewarded. In this season enjoy your accomplishments and your increase. Let go of the old, allow people to walk away.

Do: accept being promoted, stay committed to your purpose and cry, dont hold in your feelings.

Beware: of giving too much of yourself. Don't attempt to save relationships where the other person desire to depart. Don't allow feelings of abandonment and Disappointment into your heart and avoid compensating hurt feelings

Knowledge is power and intent is strategic, learn to maximize your seasons so that you can avoid setbacks. Strive to learn the lessons within each season and how to grow through them. You were designed to adapt and overcome the shift and challenge of change, your perception is everything.

Understanding the importance of accountability in these seasons are imperative, they will help you stay focused on what matter. Most people want help without accountability and answers without exposing their truth. Accountability will help you break the pattern of your failure and truth will expose the root. Regardless of your season, having consistent accountability will keep you committed to your change. Your accountability must have the necessary tools to help you. They will possess certain characteristics. You will be able to identify them because their influence in your life will always lead you back to the God source when you begin to wander.

Be careful that you don't connect with people that help to keep you, tied to your offense and married to your pain. You can't grow around people that validate your discontentment. Get around those that will challenge your perception and help you heal with truth. These are people that I call "The Power Pact"

THE POWER PACT

LION - The lion is known in nature as a Fearless creature. The lion in your life will exude a fearless nature. They are stable and consistent. This person will help you to manage your emotions helping you to address your emotional instability. They are not afraid of confrontation and will call you out on your actions.

This person is someone you can guarantee won't run. They will help you deal with and overcome passivity and push you into your victory. Their authority is evident and they have mastered the art of overcoming. They are strategist, having knowledge, understanding, and wisdom. They will help you to mature, and teach you how to be effective.

OX - The Ox is known in nature as a hard worker with great strength and endurance. The ox in your life lead by example. They are a hard worker, never expecting you to do something that they won't do. This person in your life will help you stay dedicated and committed. This person is resilient and exude strength.

Favor and blessings are attached to the ox. There is guarantee of provision when you are with them. They are significant in your life because they will be patient with you, and will build you up with words of truth and encouragement.

SHEEP - The sheep is known in nature as a follower, it has to be guided. The sheep in your life will help you stay faithful and passionate. You are able to benefit from their desire to assist and support you. This is the person that has potential, they need you to walk beside them to help them through their process.

This person is significant in your life because this person gives you purpose. They keep you accountable because they are watching and looking to you to help them to keep going. This person believes in you and they honor your presence in their life.

EAGLE - The eagle is known in nature for its ability to soar high, yet identify prey with its sharp vision. The eagle in your life is honest and trustworthy. This is the person that will help you stay integral and focused. You are able to benefit from their keen insight and wisdom.

This person is significant in your life because they will help to guide you in the right direction. They keep you aligned to your purpose and focused on the right things. This person will help you to develop and teach you how to live a life of no compromise.

The "Power Pact" will keep you motivated and encouraged to finish. Their presence in your life is critical, they will have the love, patience, and wisdom to keep you focused and consistent. The "Power Pact" will know their assignment in your life and will often remind you of their purpose in your life.

Beware of the counterfeit pact, although on the opposite of the spectrum of each other, they seemingly work together to keep you in bondage

THE COUNTERFEIT PACT

BEE - The Bee is known in nature as being busy, making their presence known by buzzing around your ears. They will sting you if they feel threatened by you. They are petty and messy, and will keep you emotionally unstable.

This person seeks to know your business and then spreads it, they are avid gossipers. The bee, help keep the pain of rejection and paranoia alive by feeding you with lies of what people said about you and manipulating you into believing them. They are seekers of information and are always in someone's business. They pretend to be about their business and getting things done.

The bee use their relationships with people as leverage, and are okay with you as long as they have your ear to feed you gossip. They seek to turn you away from people that may have a greater influence on your life than them. This person or persons never stop, they will go from one person to the next creating problems. They want to keep you down, eventually turning on you when you start to change for the better.

RAT - Known in nature as a rodent that get in where there's a crack or opening. Their presence is made known because they leave their droppings, evidence of a conspiracy between you and others. They spread plagues, causing continuous problems and distress. This person is divisive and sneaky.

This person is a perpetrator of strength, appearing to have it all together, they always have a strong opinion, but have no discipline in their own life. They look for your weaknesses and attempt to take on a role of a mentor in your life.

The rat is always plotting, looking for ways to get you off focused and away from people that can really help you. They are counterfeit helpers, wanting to draw you to themselves.

They are slanderers attempting to kill a persons character and destroy their work. They have a selfish agenda.

The rat contaminate individuals with deception, seeking out the weak in an effort to ruin their progress. They desire to keep you from growing, tempting you with your past addictions and encourage you to continue in rebellion.

SPIDER - The spider is known in nature for spinning webs to attract and trap their prey. They will suck the life out of you and leave you. This person is cunning and controlling

The spider seek to control you with false insight, they pose as a person of wisdom to draw you away from accountability. They seek to use you and entangle you in their schemes. They will tell you that others are trying to hold you back to coax you to rebel.

They are manipulators giving a lot of advice to keep you looking to them for answers. Their presence in your life is one of indirect control using their appearance of success to mesmerize you into submission with their influence, their gifts and money, to keep you around.

The spider will not submit to any type of authority although they will claim to have mentors etc., but they want you to submit to them. They are natural con artist, knowing how to get around any system. The spider live to control you and everything that's connected to you.

GOPHER - They are known in nature for digging tunnels and finding their way in. This person lacks commitment and is a destroyer of relationship. The gopher pose as a friend and as a person needing you to help them.

They will make up scenarios in an attempt to relate to you, and win your trust, often asking for your help but becoming upset at your suggestions. Gophers are passive aggressive in their relationships with people, looking for fault in you. They find your area of weakness to bring you down mentally to control and destroy you. They bring dysfunction and instability but won't take responsibility for their actions. Gophers will validate and encourage rebellion in hopes that you will fail. They want you to feel rejected so that they can pose as the only person that really care about you. Gophers always have an agenda and a motive, wanting to be the only person in your life. They look for fault in leadership and authority figures to create a revolt, lead you astray, and destroy your life.

The "Counterfeit Pact" will keep you discouraged, paranoid and wanting to quit. There presence in your life is a cancer, causing you to turn on yourself and become critical of your decisions against those who really care about you. The "Counterfeit Pact" will have constant complaints, a negative spirit, intolerance of others and a message of error, to coerce you towards destruction.

Know the difference of those that are for you and want to see you reach your destiny and those that are against you, and cause you to fall into the arms of fate.

Chapter 8

LET GO

T he beauty of a scarred heart is that it tells a story, but you determine if

the story will be one of defeat or victory, you don't have to succumb to your injuries obtained from your past. Your greatest asset and most valuable attribute is heard through your story spoken from a place of healing and not from a place of brokenness. People tend to disregard the dangers of a wounded heart, not realizing that within broken places there is a tendency to wound others from the sharpness of negative words and an ability to pierce and taint the thoughts of others with an errored perception.

HEALING

Healing adds worth to your purpose, making you qualified to assist a world in pain. Your breakthrough is not only for yourself, but it's an antidote for others, your healing is imperative. There are times when an individual may feel plagued by wounds that refuse to heal. The cause for the pause in healing may be linked to bitterness. ***Bitterness*** is a root, it's the nerve endings to your pain, it keeps the pain triggered, and it keep you victimized and sensitive. Each time that nerve is hit, it awakens, hate, regret, and self pity.

The beauty of your scars are revealed in the triumph of your story. You don't have to die a victim to your pain but you can live in the peace of forgiveness. ***Forgiveness*** is not about an apology, it's a personal decision to sever the rope that ties you to your pain by cutting off the circulation of the feelings associated with your hurt. Forgiveness is your decision to stop the surge of negativity attached to an individual from dominating your thoughts and your actions. It's choosing to stop self affliction, by disconnecting your emotions from the hurt. When you choose to forgive you are awakened to reality and released into the truth that you've had the power to take authority over your emotions all along. Your disappointment towards your past and maybe towards yourself has made you an enemy of your life, precipitating you to subconsciously rob yourself of joy and sabotage your progress and impair your life.

The grace to let go is released when you decide to live in peace, on purpose, and with progression. Your success is tied to your decision to reevaluate and adjust your view and align your life. You will benefit from discovering purpose, but you must look for it. Your purpose is a treasure that's hidden beneath the remains of your tragedy, explore your sea of pain that wreaked you, to find your value. Make an alliance with your past and your future to become greater than you've been. Life in retrospect as a means to heal, will help you see the meaning in what you've been through and it will assist you in letting go.

The clarification of letting go is just as important as the will to let go. Letting go is synonymous to throwing up. It's breaking up/divorcing the person, place, or thing that's kept you tied and in bondage and *utilizing* your knowledge of hurts presence in your life as leverage to search for its roots. It's *applying* your understanding of hurts aide in keeping the pain alive to purposefully walk through the process of *eliminating* the negative associations stored in your memory through unforgiveness.

Freeing yourself of self infliction and torment is in the acceptance that the pain started in your past and was suppose to be left in the past, you have a future to show up for. Leave your pain by *disconnecting* from the emotions that keep the pain alive, accept that your past happened, but welcome the lesson learned to become better. Many of our mistakes are tied to not having a matured mind to make the right decisions in moments but, most of our victories are tied to having a renewed mind to know how to make better decisions in the future. Letting go is difficult when an individual choose to hide their hurt and refuse to admit their wrong. You can't change the past, but you can show up in your future, changed, and willing to invest in the maintenance of wholeness.

Healing is a choice, that must happen inwardly. Your outward response to the pain will change when your mind and your emotions change towards the pain. This is not an easy task considering the years that people have spent practicing how not to wear their pain, hiding from the real effects that their past has had on their life. Many have mastered faking it and have managed to keep who they've become inwardly, concealed, making healing difficult because of the fear of appearing broken.

Often, we become comfortable with managing our emotions and never dealing with them. There must be a shift from suppressive behaviors as a means to cope and transition into proactive behaviors as a means to heal, you have to choose to go through the process. It will be hard but you must continuously speak and declare over yourself, life. You can heal, you will heal, and you want to heal. Confess healing everyday until you process your past pain, completely.

Healing is painful, walking through your past will force things that you have buried to resurface, this is why it's important to have your "Power Pact" that will help you walk through the process. Allow them access to your fears, they will help you to conquer them. The journey towards healing will hurt more in the beginning but the pain will subside overtime as you continue in your process of healing. You may be left with a scar, reminding you of your past but the scar is proof of healing. Be cautious not to despise your scar to the extent that you reopen it.

Healing is intentional, confrontation precede healing. Be willing to address your pained past, you will reap the benefit of healing. Healing is introducing your problem to the solution and implementing that solution until you see results. Its being willing to pursue change until your change come.

Healing is progressive, Lasting change is a process. Healing is a journey of consistent intent and planned persistence. Healing takes time because it involves adjusting your thoughts to think different of your life. Practice positive thinking to align your will to purpose. Your desire to be whole has to be greater than your desire to stay stuck.

Healing is work, Having faith for change without working your faith to change will only make you discouraged and frustrated. Be willing to do something about the state that you are in. It's a journey of choices, a daily renewal of your thoughts and your actions. You have to put in the work towards healing to reap the benefit of healing, the extent of your willingness to work through your pain, determines your outcome. Don't be afraid to *feel* the discomforts of healing, stop running away and **face it**, you must resist the fear of returning back to a vulnerable place, and know that you have a purpose to prosper.

Choose to *Learn* the lessons so that you can pass the tests of time, you will have more disappointments and more experiences in your life, but when you've learned from your past, you won't ever repeat it. There may be situations that look like what you've already experienced but your response to the pressure of those moments should not look like your past. Don't be afraid to question how you feel in a moment, you must become attuned with your environment and your emotions to identify triggers. Healing send you into a learning curve and requires patience.

During the process of healing, learn how to accept the imperfections of life and the flaws in your processing. It's important that you avoid placing limits on yourself because you are afraid of failing. *Embrace* your weaknesses so that you can discover your strength. Remind yourself that you are changing and that the uncomfortability of change is healthy. It's okay to become frustrated with the process, but you must keep going. Avoid lingering in *Disappointment*, it is a setup for stagnation it will trap you in seasons, and keep you mentally, emotionally and physically in places where you should have progressed.

When you have chosen to heal, you are choosing to let go of not just pain, but the hindrances and tactics we use to avoid dealing with our pain. You can't have a fear of letting go. Your past pain was never meant to be your identity. We often hide ourselves within the damage of our past, using it as a security blanket, it becomes the excuse we use not to change. The fear of letting go is entangled in an identity that's false, but the security in the false identity comes from avoidance. Most people would prefer to keep things as they are to avoid the work associated with change. Although an individual's standards and beliefs may be a result to their experience, they feel a sense of control in refusing to change and that it's easier to remain submissive to a false identity.

Many individuals tend to use *Buffers*, to deliberately distract them from dealing with the issue at hand. The buffers will cause an individual to start projects, to prevent them from dealing with a problem. Buffers are a form of *Avoidance*, its a learned behavior embedded within our actions to keep us from finishing. When change start to happen our internal conflicts of confusion, fear, and doubt, want to abort the process. This can start a war of conflicting behaviors that exhaust you back into old pattern behaviors. These conflicting behaviors eventually become permanent stumbling blocks, keeping an individual preoccupied doing other things.

Letting go must become a matter of willfully turning over your desire to cope for the strength to heal, refusing to allow your excuses to keep you bound. Your fight has to become stronger than your excuses. There must be a tenacity and courage to fight and you must have the power to endure, you need God. It's imperative that we don't confuse the human intelligence with the majesty of the creator. Our acknowledgement of the creator, repositions us in a place of being pliable, where our thoughts and actions, can be renewed and refurbished. The tools provided up to this point are designed to assist you in your process with knowledge and understanding, however the power to change can only come from God. You must lean on the greater source of strength to help you maintain stability. We all have a measure of ability gifted to us to overcome, but our ability to master and mitigate the struggles associated with changing, need a power greater than ourselves.

Know and believe that there is a power greater than you, that has kept you, even in your ignorance of not understanding this greater powers role in your life. This power source has always been at work in our life. The clarification of that source is just as important as your belief in the power that's greater than you. Many acknowledge the existence of other powers and created beings, but one must understand the importance of the specification of the creator God, Jehovah-Bara, who is Yahweh the self existing one. He is also El Roi, the God who sees and remembers you, and El Shaddai the overpowerer over every spirit of defeatism and He is Elohim, the God of heavens army that fights for you. The characteristic of the right God source assures you of God's ability to help you. The truth of His power is a change agent, having the ability to reroute your life. It's God who gives your past pain a future, and demand the pain of your past to become a stream of wealth. God will show you how to cash out on your pain and live off the fruit of it. This wealthy stream is hidden within the lessons you've learned and your decision to let go. Its God, that show up through your scars and reveal that you triumphed over death, and what was meant to kill you couldn't. Its God that gives you hope in the midst of your tragedy and turns it into your testimony.

True change start the moment you decide to change. Its the beginning to your tomorrow, with understanding the God source that rules the day, and the spirit of God that empowers your way. True change happens within your moment of surrender of your spirit, soul and body. The establishment of God's mandate for your life, the acceptance of Jesus Christ as the mediator between you and God and the acceptance of a right spirit in your actions and in your will, is the rotor that reestablishes your life, and repositions you. There must be a plight of submission where you enter into a covenant relationship with God, being willing to trust His way over yours. It's not a matter of religion, nor about entering into the demands of a religion, but its about entering into a partnering relationship with your creator, learning the ways of your design, and how to get the most out of your life. Its choosing the way less followed and committing to...

1. Willfully and Fearlessly convert to a new way. (God knows your capabilities)
2. Willfully let go of negative people, places, and things, your sanity is more important (when you gain strength, God will restore necessary things and relationships)
3. Willfully submit to God's way. The Word of God as written in the Holy Bible is a Blueprint to how we are to live. Get understanding of it and refuse to compromise and deviate from His Word as it is rightfully interpreted. (Having the correct understanding is key, you must be able to properly contextualize the Word of God. Seek to understand it, getting help if needed)
4. Refuse to give up. Know that God cares about you, and your situation, and because He cares He will help you through it all.

Letting go must essentially become your starting point as well as your ending, this process of healing requires daily exchange, where you are letting go of perceptions and ideologies. Before you are able to apply the fundamentals of change, you must have the right foundational truth. Salvation through Jesus, the son of God is foundational, the life that Jesus lead was a life boundless and stable, He knew who He was and He stayed true to His identity and His purpose. The teachings of Jesus provided a compass for life yielding strategies and principles to live by, He was faithful and committed to the Father, God. The power of Jesus released a greater meaning to all who came in contact with Him. In His presence was healing and deliverance. The sacrifice of Jesus provided hope for all people, He was willing to give His life so that we could live with a choice, to live a life of defeat, accepting our fate, or to live a life of victory through Him, accepting our destiny to be prosperous.

Empowerment through the Spirit of God is the endowment needed to give us the ability to change, the guidance that lead us to the right people and to the right places for change, the power to change and the ability to live a life of change. The beauty of a life that welcomes salvation is the assurance of a life changed, regardless of your situation, your age, your culture etc., Salvation becomes the bridge that anyone can cross if they choose and faith becomes the substance that fills the empty place in the heart with meaning.

In your endeavors to experience freedom and relief understand that living a progressive life is a choice that you must make everyday. Our inability to save ourselves must be countered with the knowledge of God's ability and desire to save us. Many mistaken salvation as a one time decision, neglecting the maintenance of a life surrendered to God. Each day you must make a choice to choose Him to rule your day. You must walk in humility, not thinking more of yourself then you ought. You are who you are because of who the creator made you to be. You are not greater then the next creation, each of us have a function and purpose. Make prayer a priority, talk to God, He is omnipresent meaning that He is present everywhere. Our relationship with God is spiritual, it takes understanding the spiritual aspects of life to take advantage of incorporating a life of daily talks. Talking to God, is the position you take when you are attempting to work through a problem. Speak out loud so that you can hear yourself in the hope of gaining a greater understanding, instead of just thinking it. Our conversations with God is one of intimate ponder and internal prompting, it ignites a deeper seek within us. This search to understand more deeply is a key component in your maturity. You will be able to see God at work in your life. Keep your heart guarded and turn away from things that make you susceptible to internal conflict, things that will cause guilt, shame, and regret. Surround yourself with positivity to assure that you remain optimistic in your journey.

Learn the lifestyle and practice the ways of an individual determined to see change. Stay in tuned to what work and what doesn't. Measure your outcome not based on how you feel, but in the truth of the process. You have what you need to overcome every obstacle. Though your pains past was the door opened that prevented you from having the life you desired, your pains future will be the success of a life worth living. Your pain had a past but now it has a future.

CPSIA information can be obtained
at www.ICGtesting.com
Printed in the USA
LVHW041203170520
655737LV00005B/426